PLANET
EARTH

Robin Kerrod

Lerner Publications Company • Minneapolis

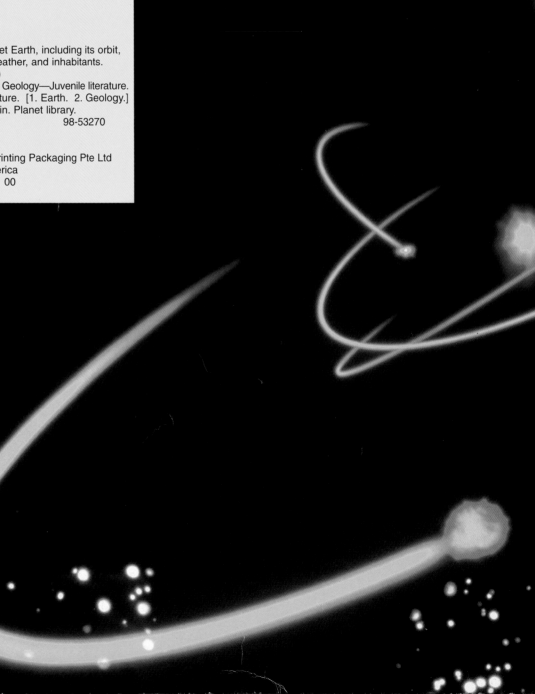

This edition published in 2000

Lerner Publications Company
A Division of Lerner Publishing Group
241 First Avenue North, Minneapolis MN 55401 U.S.A.

Website address: www.lernerbooks.com

© 2000 by Graham Beehag Books

Library of Congress Cataloging-in-Publication Data

Kerrod, Robin.
    Planet Earth / Robin Kerrod.
       p. cm. – (Planet library)
    Includes index.
    Summary: Introduces the planet Earth, including its orbit, geology, oceans, atmosphere, weather, and inhabitants.
    ISBN 0-8225-3902-0 (lib. bdg.)
    1. Earth—Juvenile literature. 2. Geology—Juvenile literature.
3. Geophysics—Juvenile literature. [1. Earth. 2. Geology.]
I. Title. II. Series: Kerrod, Robin. Planet library.
QB631.4.K47   2000   98-53270
550—dc21

Printed in Singapore by Tat Wei Printing Packaging Pte Ltd
Bound in the United States of America
1 2 3 4 5 6 – OS – 05 04 03 02 01 00

CONTENTS

Introducing Planet Earth

Earth is the planet on which we live. It is part of the solar system, or family of bodies that travel around the Sun. Earth circles the Sun along with eight other planets. As planets go, Earth is fairly small—its diameter, or distance through Earth from North Pole to South Pole, is less than one-tenth the diameter of Jupiter. But Earth's diameter is more than five times that of the smallest planet, Pluto.

Earth formed at the same time as the other planets, about 4.6 billion years ago. It is made up mainly of different kinds of rock. About 70 percent of Earth's surface is covered by water. Land areas cover the rest. The land areas form the continents, and the water areas form the oceans.

Earth is also surrounded by gases. The gases form a layer around Earth called the atmosphere. One of the gases in the atmosphere is oxygen. This is the gas almost all animals must breathe in order to stay alive.

Plant and animal life thrives on Earth in millions of different forms on the land, in the oceans, and in the air. Conditions on Earth are just right for life. Water and air are available, and temperatures are comfortable because Earth is not too close to and not too far away from the Sun.

As far as we know, Earth is the only planet in our solar system that has living things. Indeed, it is the only place in the universe that we know has living things.

From space, Earth looks blue because of its oceans. This photograph shows the continent of Africa, with the Atlantic Ocean on the left and the Indian Ocean on the right.

Our Home Planet

Earth is one of the four small, rocky inner planets that lie close to the Sun. Like all planets, Earth travels around the Sun, and it turns around like a top.

Earth is the third planet out from the Sun, which lies about 93 million miles (150 million km) away. Earth's nearest neighbors among the planets are Venus, Mars, and Mercury. They are made up mainly of rock, like Earth. These four inner planets are called the terrestrial, or Earth-like, planets.

SPEEDING THROUGH SPACE

Every day we see the Sun travel slowly across the sky. Every night we see the stars wheel slowly overhead. Earth seems to stand still. But the opposite is true. The Sun and the other stars only seem to move. In fact, they stand still and Earth moves. Earth is turning around in space like a top. It takes one day for Earth to turn, or rotate, all the way around on its axis. An axis is an imaginary line running through a planet from its north pole to its south pole.

At the same time that it rotates, Earth also travels through space in a path, or orbit, that takes it around the Sun. It orbits all the way around the Sun in a little over 365 days, a period we call one year.

Earth is different from the other rocky planets because most of the rocky surface is covered by the water of the oceans.

Earth orbits the Sun between Venus and Mars. On average, it lies about 93 million miles (150 million km) from the Sun.

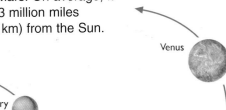

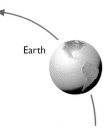

Mars

Earth

Venus

Mercury

Sun

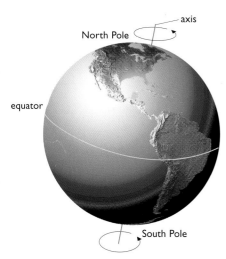

Earth spins around an imaginary line called the axis. The equator is another imaginary line midway between the North and South Poles.

THE BIG ATTRACTION

Like the other planets, Earth is spherical, or shaped like a ball. But it is not perfectly round. It bulges a little around the equator, which is an imaginary line around Earth, midway between the North and South Poles.

Earth weighs more than 6,000,000,000,000,000,000,000 tons. Like every other massive object, Earth has a powerful attraction, or pull. We call this pull gravity. Gravity is what keeps our feet firmly on the ground and what makes objects fall when we drop them.

Earth's force of gravity also reaches out into the space around it. Earth's gravity holds the Moon in its orbit around our planet.

Earth's Companion

Earth travels through space with a close companion—the Moon. The Moon lies on average about 239,000 miles (384,000 km) away. This seems like a long way, but it's only a small step in space.

The Moon is Earth's only natural satellite. A satellite is a smaller object orbiting around a larger one. The Moon is a different world from Earth. It is drab in color, has no oceans, no atmosphere, and no life.

Earth and its Moon are pictured together in a photograph taken by the *Galileo* space probe.

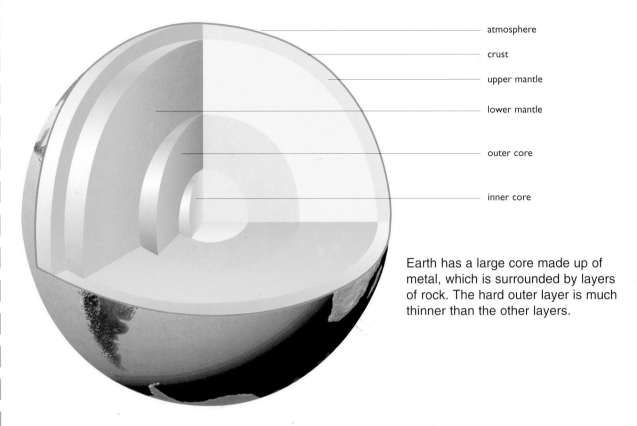

atmosphere
crust
upper mantle
lower mantle
outer core
inner core

Earth has a large core made up of metal, which is surrounded by layers of rock. The hard outer layer is much thinner than the other layers.

EARTH DATA

Diameter at equator: 7,926 miles (12,756 km)

Diameter at poles: 7,900 miles (12,714 km)

Average distance from Sun: 93,000,000 miles (150,000,000 km)

Rotates in: 23 hours 56 minutes

Orbits Sun in: 365¼ days

Moons: 1 (the Moon)

WHAT EARTH IS MADE OF

Scientists who study Earth are called geologists. The word *geologist* comes from *Geos*, the Latin word for Earth. From their studies, geologists have found that Earth is made up of several layers.

The center part of Earth is called the core. The core is extremely hot and is made up of different kinds of metal. The main metals are iron and nickel. In Earth's center, in the inner core, the metals are solid. But in the outer part of the core, the metals are liquid. No one has gotten near Earth's core, but scientists believe it may get as hot as 11,000° F (6,100° C).

Outside the core is a thick rock layer called the mantle. The rock in the mantle is made up of materials such as magnesium, iron, and silicon. The part of the mantle closest to the core is soft. This soft rock can flow slowly, like hot tar on a road. But the outer part of the mantle is hard and rigid. Although the mantle reaches high temperatures, it is not nearly as hot as Earth's core.

The outermost layer of Earth is made up of a thin layer of rock. This hard rock is called the crust, and it's made of materials such as granite, shale, and marble. We cannot always see the crust because much of it lies under the oceans or is covered by soft ground and plants. The crust is about 25 miles (40 km) thick on land, but only about 6 miles (10 km) thick under the oceans.

Right: Earth is constantly rebuilding itself from the inside through volcanic eruptions. Liquid rock flows from beneath Earth's crust, and solid rock is formed by cooling.

Shocking Methods

Geologists learn about what Earth is like inside by studying waves that move through it during earthquakes. Earthquakes are shakings in underground rock caused by movement inside Earth. These shakings send out ripples called shock waves. The waves travel all through Earth. Scientists in different parts of the world record when the waves reach them and trace the path of the shock waves through Earth. Scientists find that the waves bend at certain depths. The waves bend where they meet a different layer of rock. By studying how the waves bend, scientists can tell where each layer of Earth begins and ends.

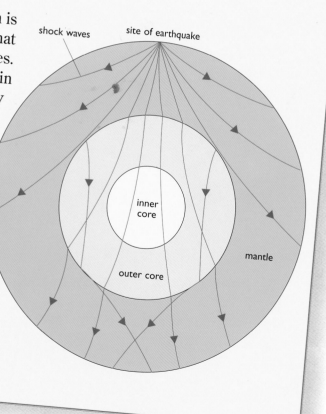

Drifting Continents

Earth's surface is not a solid slab of rock. It is made up of many different pieces, like a jigsaw puzzle. All these pieces are moving very slowly, causing continents to drift, oceans to widen, and mountains to form.

The Atlantic Ocean is about 35 feet (11 m) wider today than it was when Christopher Columbus first crossed it in 1492.

If you look at a map of the Atlantic Ocean and the continents on each side, you might notice something. South America looks as if it might fit like a puzzle piece with Africa. And North America looks as if it might fit with Europe in the same way.

In fact, scientists are certain that these continents were joined together a long time ago. But over time, the continents have slowly drifted apart, and the Atlantic Ocean has come between them. This kind of movement is called continental drift, and it happens all over Earth's surface.

There are many examples of evidence of continental drift. For instance, deposits from glaciers that existed hundreds of millions of years ago have been found in warm places such as India, Australia, Africa, and South America. The glacial deposits probably mean that these continents were once in a cold place, possibly close to the South Pole. In the same way, certain fossils found in North America show that our continent was probably once near the equator. Fossils are the remains of living things.

MOVING PLATES

To understand how continental drift takes place, think about the way Earth is made up. The crust and top part of the mantle are solid rock. But the rock layer underneath is soft. Heat from deeper down in the mantle makes the soft rock hot and starts it moving, just like a radiator starts warm air moving in a room. As the soft rock layer moves, it causes

150 million years ago

100 million years ago

This map of the world shows the seven large plates and several smaller ones that make up Earth's surface. The red lines show the boundaries between the plates, and the arrows show the directions in which the plates are moving.

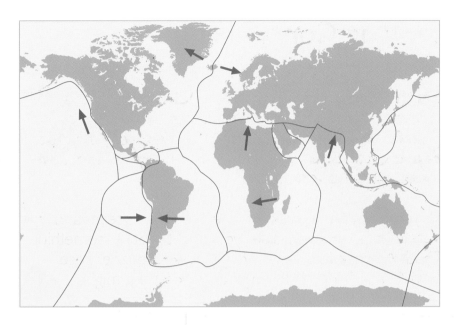

slabs of the hard rock above it to move. Scientist call these slabs plates.

The map above shows the main plates that make up Earth's surface. Most of the continents sit on separate plates. The main boundaries between plates are located in the middle of the oceans.

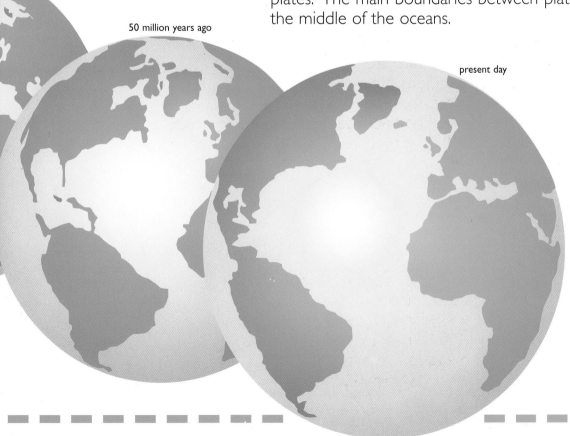

50 million years ago

present day

These drawings show how the surface of our planet has changed over time.

This picture shows the northern part of the Red Sea. The sea is slowly getting wider due to sea-floor spreading.

THE SPREADING SEAS

The continents are not the only parts of Earth's surface that are moving. The ocean floors move as well. In most oceans, the floor is moving in different directions in different places. For example, the eastern and western parts of the Atlantic Ocean floor sit on different plates that are moving in opposite directions. This means that the ocean floor is spreading apart.

Plates are spreading apart in many parts of the ocean floor. Where this is happening, molten, or liquid, rock pushes its way upward from deep underground. As the molten rock comes up, it spreads east and west. Then it cools and fills in the gap between the existing plates. The cooled rock will in turn be forced to spread apart by new molten rock forcing its way upward. This process is called sea-floor spreading.

Where sea-floor spreading is happening, a mountain range forms underwater. The build-up of new plate material forms underwater ridges along plate bounderies. A mountain range like this runs down the middle of the Atlantic Ocean and is called the Mid-Atlantic Ridge.

Below: Movements in hot rock underneath solid plates cause the plates to shift. When plates push against each other in the middle of a land mass (as at left), they push the land in between upward, creating mountains. When molten rock wells up through the ocean floor (as at right), new plate material forms along a mid-ocean ridge.

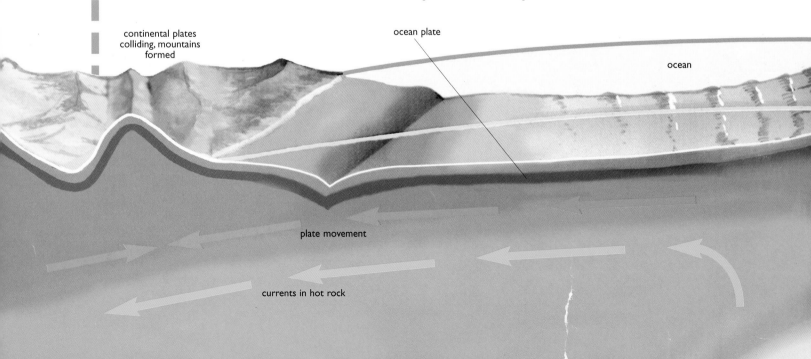

continental plates colliding, mountains formed

ocean plate

ocean

plate movement

currents in hot rock

SPLITTING CONTINENTS

Sometimes molten rock pushes its way upward through a continent. The molten rock forces the continent to split apart. This process is happening in the Great Rift Valley in Africa. In time, the valley will widen and become flooded with the sea. Then a new ocean will form and grow wider and wider.

WHEN PLATES COLLIDE

New plate material is constantly forming and spreading out in the middle of the oceans. But in other places, plate material is being destroyed. This happens when two plates collide with each other. One plate dips below the other and returns to Earth's interior, melting as it does so.

When an ocean plate collides with a continental plate, the ocean plate dips down. The continental plate rides up over it. This causes the land to wrinkle up and form a mountain range. Rock in the ocean plate melts and may force its way up through the range to form volcanoes. The Andes Mountains on the western edge of South America were formed in this way and have many volcanoes.

The Himalayas are the highest mountain range on Earth. The mountains formed when two plates collided.

Below: When plates collide at the ocean edge, the ocean plate is forced downward. A trench forms under the sea, while the land wrinkles up to form mountains, often with volcanoes.

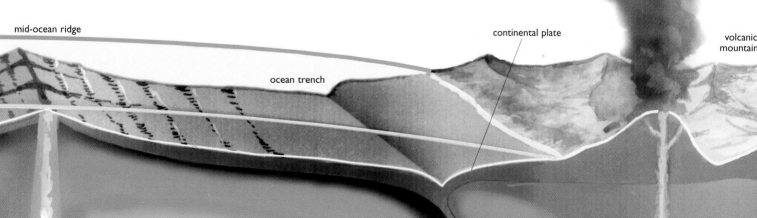

mid-ocean ridge

ocean trench

continental plate

volcanic mountains

Volcanoes and Earthquakes

Movement of the plates that make up Earth's crust can cause volcanic eruptions and earthquakes. Both are among nature's most amazing spectacles, and they can be extremely dangerous.

In Hawaii, molten lava pours over the rocks like a fiery waterfall. It is coming from Kilauea, one of the most active volcanoes on Earth.

When a volcano erupts, great fountains of red-hot liquid rock called lava spurt out through an opening in Earth's crust. Volcanoes also send out great clouds of ash. Lava pours out and runs along the ground in fiery rivers. After lava cools, it turns into hard rock. Most volcanoes erupt many times over a long period of time. Volcanoes gradually grow into mountains, as layers of lava rock build up.

There are hundreds of volcanoes around the edge of the plates beneath the Pacific Ocean. They form what is called the Ring of Fire. Other volcanoes have formed in places such as Hawaii, Iceland, and Africa.

Vesuvius and Pompeii

The most famous volcanic eruption in history took place in the year A.D. 79, when Mount Vesuvius erupted in Italy. Its billowing ash cloud buried the nearby town of Pompeii and killed thousands of people. At the time, Pompeii was one of the most magnificent cities in the Roman Empire. After the eruption, the city lay forgotten for nearly 1,700 years. Excavations of the ruins began over 50 years ago, uncovering ancient buildings, streets, and even the remains of humans buried by the ash from Mount Vesuvius.

A view from above the excavated remains of Pompeii

This town in Italy has been devastated by a severe earthquake. Nearly every year, earthquakes kill large numbers of people, and destroy many homes around the world.

Volcanic eruptions can cause destruction, but the lava they produce also creates new land. Some volcanic eruptions that occur on the ocean floor produce enough lava to eventually form large mounds that rise out of the water and become islands. The Hawaiian Islands began to form in this way about 30 million years ago.

On land, many small and large mountains were once erupting volcanoes. Mount Rainier, the largest mountain in the state of Washington, formed from a volcano. After the volcano became inactive, or stopped erupting, plant and animal life began to inhabit the newly formed land.

THE SHAKING EARTH

Like volcanic eruptions, most earthquakes take place along the edges of plates. When plates move over or past one another, they do not move smoothly. Their edges are rough and often lock together. The plates try to move but cannot. Pressure builds up in the rocks until they give way, and the plates move with a sudden jerk. This makes the rocks shake, causing an earthquake.

An earthquake produces tremors, or waves, that travel through the underground rocks to the surface. When the waves reach the surface, they can cause enormous destruction. They shake houses to pieces, split roads apart, and hurt or kill large numbers of people. In the 1976 earthquake in Tangshan, China, as many as 250,000 people perished.

This satellite picture of the coast of California shows the famous San Andreas Fault. A fault is a fracture in Earth's crust where sections of rock are rubbing against each other. This fault has been responsible for many earthquakes. It runs from the bottom right to the top left of the picture.

Earth Rocks

Many kinds of rock make up Earth's crust, both on land and beneath the sea. Some rocks formed when molten rock cooled and became solid. Others formed from material that settled in the bottom of ancient rivers and seas.

Most of Earth's rocks are made of one or more minerals. Minerals are solid substances in the earth that are not part of plants or animals. Each mineral is made up of a separate element or a combination of elements. There are three main kinds of rock on Earth—igneous, sedimentary, and metamorphic. Each kind of rock is formed in a different way.

COOLED ROCK

Granite is an example of what is called an igneous rock. The word *igneous* means formed by fire. Granite forms when magma, or hot liquid rock, cools and becomes solid under the ground. It cools slowly, and this allows the minerals in it to grow coarse crystals.

Basalt is another common kind of igneous rock that forms from magma. Basalt is formed when magma has found its way to the surface through a volcano. On the surface, it cools quickly, and the minerals it contains have little time to grow. This is why basalt contains only very tiny crystals.

As certain igneous rocks cool, mineral crystals, such as the tourmaline crystal above, form in the rocks.

Basalt and granite are two of the most common rocks found in Earth's crust. They are both igneous rocks.

basalt

granite

slate

Slate is a metamorphic rock. It formed from a sedimentary rock called shale. Then heat and pressure changed the shale into slate.

Layers of Time

By studying the different layers in sedimentary rocks and the fossils they contain, geologists can piece together a detailed geological history of Earth. Geologists can tell approximately when the layers were formed, and this gives them the geological time scale. It begins about 600 million years ago, at the time when fossils began appearing in large quantities in the rocks. Geological time is divided into intervals called eras and periods.

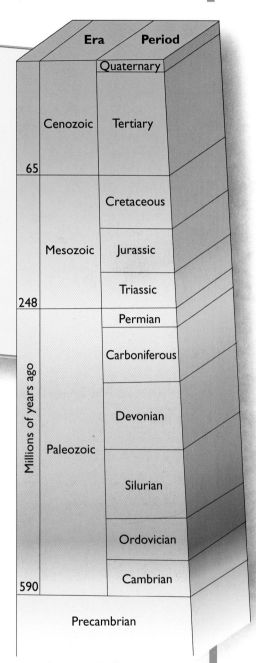

LAYERED ROCKS

Other kinds of rock are formed from materials such as mud and sand. These materials are washed off the land by rivers and settle in the bottom of ancient seas. The settled material is called sediment. Layers of sediment build up and become pressed together. Over time, the layers turn into solid rock. We call this kind of rock sedimentary rock.

Common sedimentary rocks are shale, which forms from layers of mud, and sandstone, which forms from layers of sand. Some kinds of sedimentary rock formed when ancient seas dried up and left behind the chemicals that were dissolved in them. Limestone is a common example. Chalk is made up of the same chemical. But it is made up of fossils, or the remains of tiny creatures that lived and died in the ancient seas.

CHANGED ROCKS

A third kind of rock is called metamorphic rock. The word *metamorphic* means having to do with change. Metamorphic rocks are rocks that have been changed by heat and pressure underground. Slate and marble are common metamorphic rocks. Slate was once shale, and marble was once limestone.

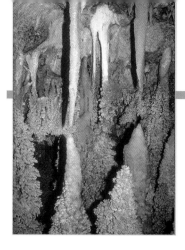

Stalagmites rise from the floor and stalactites hang from the roof of a limestone cave.

Erosion created the Grand Canyon in Arizona. For millions of years, the Colorado River has been cutting into the rocks so that in places the Canyon is a mile (1.6 km) deep. The layers in the sides of the Canyon tell us that the rocks are sedimentary.

The Changing Landscape

The face of Earth is constantly changing due to many forces, including the weather, water, wind, and glaciers. Even the highest mountains will eventually be worn down into little hills.

The wearing away of Earth's surface is known as erosion. It is going on all the time. Weather plays a major part in the process, attacking Earth with rain, snow, cold, and heat. Over time, weather breaks down and loosens rock from Earth's surface. This stage of the erosion process is called weathering.

Changes in temperature help cause weathering. During the day, the heat from the Sun makes the outer layers of rocks expand rapidly. At night, they cool down quickly and shrink. This constant expanding and shrinking eventually causes the layers to flake off. Frost has a similar effect. It freezes water that has trickled into tiny holes in the rocks. The water expands as it freezes into ice, and in time it forces off flakes of rock.

ATTACK BY WATER

The landscape is attacked by water in a number of ways. Mountain streams flow swiftly and carry along stones that scrape the rocks in the riverbed. Streams and rivers also gradually dissolve away some of the minerals in the rocks that they flow through.

When river water attacks limestone, it hollows out deep channels and caves in the rock. In these caves, the constant dripping of water creates great stone "icicles" that hang from the roof. Drippings from the icicles create columns on the floor. We call the icicles stalactites and the columns stalagmites.

Rivers play another important part in erosion. They help transport material formed

Humans Changing Earth's Surface

The human race is also changing the face of Earth. Farming, logging, and overgrazing by livestock all cause Earth's crust to erode. For instance, using plows to farm land loosens soil and breaks it down. The soil is then more easily blown or washed away. Logging forest trees also causes erosion. When trees are removed, they no longer hold down the soil and protect it from rain. In the same way, overgrazing by livestock destroys the grass and other plants that hold down soil.

Humans are destroying vast expanses of rain forest every year.

by weathering, such as mud and sand. Most often, rivers carry this material, known as sediment, into the sea.

Waves from the sea help push pieces of rock and sand onto sandy beaches. At rocky shorelines, the waves carry particles that crash into rock formations. The force of the waves carves out arches and caves in the rock.

ATTACK BY WIND

In desert regions, wind is a major cause of erosion. It picks up particles of sand and flings them against rocks. This sandblasting gradually wears away the rocks.

ATTACK BY ICE

Glaciers are another cause of erosion. A glacier is a large body of ice and snow that moves very slowly down mountains or over land. Glaciers form in cold places, such as near the North and South Poles, and in high mountains. As it moves across land, a glacier carries broken rock and scrapes away soil in its path.

The Mississippi River dumps about 500 million tons of sediment into the sea every year. The sediment has built up to form an area of land called the Mississippi Delta where the Mississippi empties into the Gulf of Mexico.

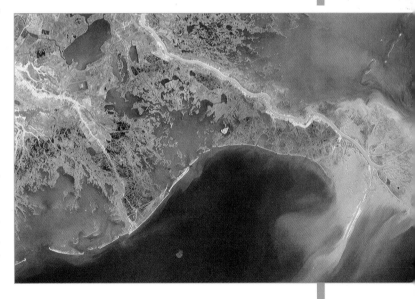

The Watery Earth

Most of Earth's surface is covered by the water of the oceans. The largest oceans are the Pacific, the Atlantic, and the Indian Oceans. The Pacific Ocean is twice as big as the Atlantic and covers about a third of Earth's surface.

Atlantic Ocean

Pacific Ocean

The water in the oceans has many chemicals dissolved in it and tastes salty. The main chemical in ocean water is sodium chloride, which is the same as ordinary salt we use at home.

Fresh water, which does not contain salt, is found in rivers and lakes on land. It is also found in high mountains and at the North and South Poles in the form of ice. There are traces of fresh water in the air in the form of water vapor.

Water remains permanently frozen as ice near the North Pole.

Waves that have traveled across oceans can grow to a great height when they reach the shore.

The Ocean Surface

Waves ripple across the ocean surface most of the time. They are created by the wind. In stormy weather, when winds blow strongly, waves can rise up to more than 40 feet (12 m) high.

Winds also cause great currents of water to flow through the oceans. These currents follow the same path year after year. There are warm currents and cold currents. One of the best-known warm currents is the Gulf Stream in the Atlantic Ocean. It travels north along the East Coast of the United States. Westerly winds that blow toward north-western Europe are warmed as they cross the Gulf Stream. These warmed winds help to create mild temperatures in nortwestern Europe.

The level of the water in the oceans does not stay the same. Twice a day, the level rises and falls. This movement is called the tides. Tides are caused by the gravity of the Moon. As the Moon passes over an ocean, it tugs at the water on Earth. This makes the water level rise and causes a high tide. When the Moon moves on, the water level falls to a low tide.

STAR POINT

On average, the oceans are about 2½ miles (4 km) deep. At its deepest point, the Marianas Trench in the Pacific Ocean is nearly 7 miles (11 km) deep.

A lightship is stranded ashore at low tide. In a few hours, the tide will flow back in and refloat the ship. Along some coasts, the tide rises and falls as much as 50 feet (15 m). Along others, the tide hardly changes at all.

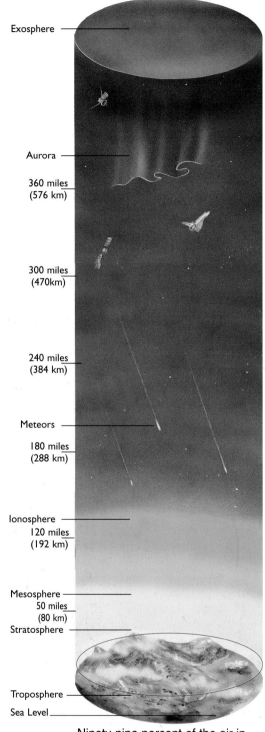

Exosphere

Aurora

360 miles
(576 km)

300 miles
(470km)

240 miles
(384 km)

Meteors

180 miles
(288 km)

Ionosphere
120 miles
(192 km)

Mesosphere
50 miles
(80 km)
Stratosphere

Troposphere
Sea Level

Ninety-nine percent of the air in
Earth's atmosphere is found in the
bottom two layers, the troposphere
and the stratosphere.

Earth's Atmosphere

The layer of air around and above us makes life possible on Earth. It gives us oxygen to breathe, it helps keep us warm, and it protects us from dangerous rays from outer space.

The layer of gases we call the atmosphere, or air, is a mixture of many gases. Only two gases are present in large amounts. One is nitrogen, which makes up 78 percent of our air. The other is oxygen, which makes up 21 percent. Other gases are present in only very small amounts. They include argon, carbon dioxide, helium, and sulfur dioxide.

Earth's atmosphere stretches to a height of about 400 miles (650 km) above the surface of Earth. The air is thickest near Earth's surface because of the weight of all the air above it. The air becomes thinner higher up. Eventually, the atmosphere fades away into outer space.

The atmosphere is divided into a number of different layers. The bottom layer is called the troposphere. This is where most of our weather happens. The troposphere is about 12 miles (18 km) thick near the equator, but only about 5 miles (8 km) thick near the North and South Poles.

THE OUTER LAYERS

The next layer up is the stratosphere, which extends to a height of about 30 miles (48 km). Within the stratosphere is a thin layer of a gas called ozone. The ozone layer is very important to life on Earth because it blocks most of the dangerous ultraviolet rays that come from the Sun. Too much exposure to ultraviolet rays can burn our skin.

The mesosphere is above the stratosphere and extends to about 50 miles (80 km) above Earth. Temperatures are extremely low in this layer. Parts of the mesosphere can be as cold as −100° F (−73° C).

The uppermost layer in Earth's atmosphere is the thermosphere. The air in the thermosphere is extremely thin and grows thinner as it extends toward outer space. The lower part of the thermosphere is called the ionosphere. In the ionosphere, air is present in the form of ions, or electrically charged particles. The displays of colored light we call the aurora , or Northern and Southern lights, take place in the ionosphere. It is also in this layer that meteors burn up and form fiery streaks of light.

The ionosphere reaches up to about 400 miles (650 km), where there is very little air present. In the exosphere, the upper part of the thermosphere, all traces of air disappear.

Astronauts on a space shuttle took this photograph of a sunset from space. It shows how dust in Earth's atmosphere turns the sky orange and red during a sunset.

Acid Rain

Sulfur dioxide escapes into the air naturally when volcanoes erupt. But large quantities of this gas are also produced when coal and oil are burned to produce electricity. Sulfur dioxide is a major form of air pollution. It is not only harmful to breathe, it also causes acid rain. In the atmosphere, the gas combines with moisture to form little drops of acid. This falls to Earth as acid rain. Acid rain has caused serious problems in many parts of the world. It kills life in rivers and lakes, kills trees, and attacks the stonework of buildings.

Weather and Climate

The weather on Earth changes from day to day, place to place, and season to season. The main elements that affect our weather are the air's temperature, the amount of moisture in the air, and how the air is moving.

The weather affects all our lives in so many ways that scientists study it closely. The science of the weather is called meteorology, and the people who study it are called meteorologists. They gather information about the weather from weather stations all over the world and from satellites in space. With the help of powerful computers, meteorologists try to predict how the weather will change. Then they issue a forecast that tells us what the weather will probably be like in the next few days.

TEMPERATURE

Three of the most important things meteorologists measure are temperature, pressure, and humidity. The temperature means the degree of heat or cold in the air around us. The temperature depends on how much heat each part of Earth receives from the Sun. Because Earth is round, different places receive more direct sunshine than others, and this makes some places hotter than others.

Because Earth's axis is tilted in space, different parts of Earth are tilted at different angles to the Sun throughout the year. This causes the temperature to change from season to season.

This picture of Earth has been taken by a weather satellite in infrared light to record heat. The continent of Africa stands out because it is very hot.

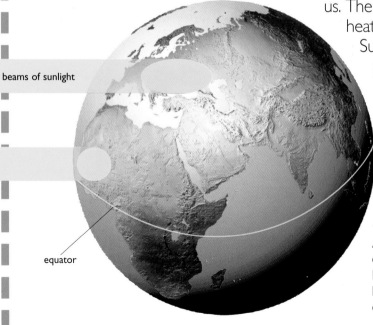

beams of sunlight

equator

A warm beam of sunlight reaches Earth most directly at the equator, so this area is always hot. Farther from the equator, sunlight becomes less direct, so temperatures grow colder to the north and south.

PRESSURE

When air becomes hot, it grows lighter and rises. When it becomes cold, it grows heavier and sinks. In the atmosphere, air is rising and sinking all around Earth. This creates air currents, or winds. The movement of large masses of warm and cold air brings about changes in the weather.

Meteorologists keep track of air movements by measuring the pressure of the air, or the force with which it presses down. When warm air rises, it produces low pressure. When cold air sinks, it produces high pressure.

HUMIDITY

Humidity is the amount of water in the air. Water is present in the air in the form of a gas we call water vapor. Water gets into the air when the Sun heats up water in the rivers and oceans and causes it to evaporate, or turn into vapor. Evaporation is part of a never-ending process in which water comes and goes between Earth's surface and the atmosphere. We call this process the water cycle.

In the water cycle, water constantly moves between Earth's surface and the atmosphere.

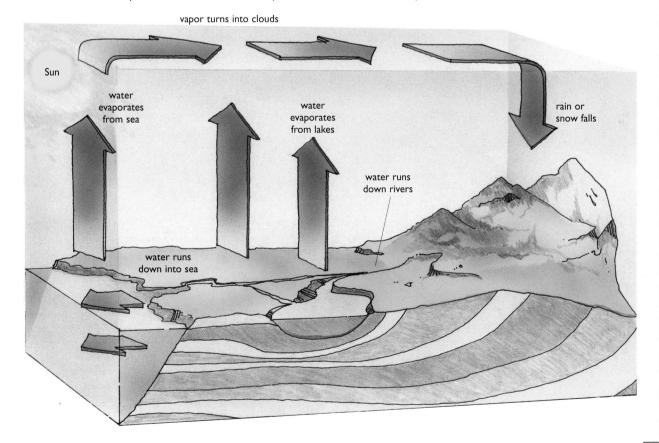

vapor turns into clouds

Sun

water evaporates from sea

water evaporates from lakes

water runs down rivers

rain or snow falls

water runs down into sea

CLOUDS, RAIN, AND SNOW

The amount of water in the air affects the weather. When a lot of water vapor is present, and the air cools down, the vapor turns into tiny water droplets. These droplets form clouds.

If the water droplets in the clouds get bigger, they fall from the clouds as rain. If the air is very cold, the droplets freeze into snow as they fall. Rain and snow are common forms of precipitation, or ways in which water in the air returns to Earth's surface. Water also returns to the ground in other ways. On cool nights, it settles out as little drops of dew. If the temperature is low, the water freezes and forms frost, which is made up of tiny ice crystals.

Top: These wispy clouds in the evening sky are called cirrus clouds. **Middle:** Tiny drops of dew have formed on this spiderweb. **Bottom:** Frost has made this feathery pattern of ice crystals.

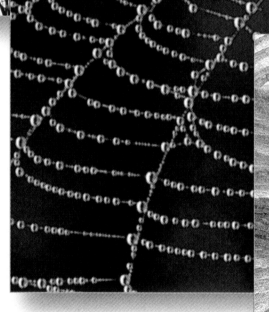

CLIMATES OF THE WORLD

As we saw earlier, different parts of Earth receive different amounts of the Sun's heat. And each part of Earth has a different pattern of weather throughout the year. We call the yearly weather pattern of a region the climate.

The map shows the world divided into eight different climatic regions, or zones. The warmest climates are found in regions near the equator, which receive the most heat from the Sun. The coldest climates are found near the North and South Poles, which receive the least heat from the Sun. Each climatic zone has its own typical plants and animals, which are suited to that climate.

Above: With thick fur, polar bears can live in the very cold Arctic climate.

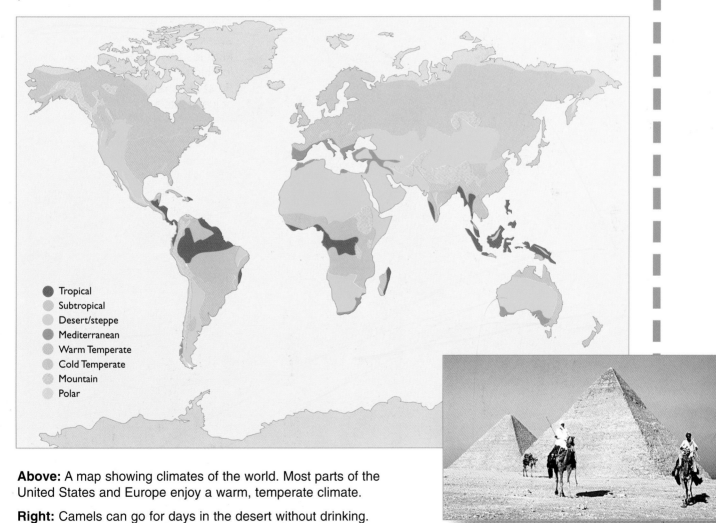

● Tropical
● Subtropical
● Desert/steppe
● Mediterranean
● Warm Temperate
● Cold Temperate
● Mountain
● Polar

Above: A map showing climates of the world. Most parts of the United States and Europe enjoy a warm, temperate climate.

Right: Camels can go for days in the desert without drinking.

Life on Earth

Earth is home to at least 1½ million different species, or kinds, of living things—plants, animals, and simpler life-forms such as bacteria. Life is found practically everywhere on Earth, from the sweltering tropics to the icy poles.

Simple forms of life first appeared on Earth billions of years ago in the early oceans. But it was not until about 600 million years ago that a real "explosion" of life began. This happened in the oceans at the start of the Cambrian period of Earth's history. Life did not appear on land until about 200 million years later. Plants appeared first, followed by insects and amphibians (animals that can live both on land and in water).

As years went by, new species appeared. By about 150 million years ago, reptiles were the main life-form. These included the dinosaurs, or

A fossil trilobite. This species lived on Earth between about 225 and 600 million years ago.

Dinosaurs roamed our planet for millions of years.

"terrible lizards." Birds also appeared around this time. About 65 million years ago, the dinosaurs and many other species died out. A new class of animals began to flourish. They were the mammals. But it may not have been until about 3 million years ago that early humans appeared on Earth.

LIVING KINGDOMS

Biologists, scientists who study living things, class life-forms, or organisms, into groups called kingdoms. The main ones are the plant and animal kingdoms. But some living things are neither plants nor animals. Fungi, such as mushrooms, are not plants because they cannot make their own food. They are placed in a separate kingdom. So are bacteria, which are microscopic organisms, or microorganisms. Other simple organisms, called protozoa (meaning "first animals"), are also placed in a separate kingdom.

PLANT LIFE

Plants are living things that can make their own food. They make food from sunlight, carbon dioxide gas from the air, and water. The process is called photosynthesis.

Like all living things, plants are made up of tiny units called cells. Certain types of algae are the simplest plants. They are very small and are made up of only a single cell. Most plants are made up of many kinds of cells.

Fungi

Dryad's Saddle

Fly Agaric

Morel

Algae

Flowering plants, such as these sunflowers, are complex plants made up of many kinds of cells.

Animals of all shapes and sizes populate Earth, from lumbering elephants **(top)** and graceful birds like the bald eagle **(center)**, to humans. All humans belong to the same animal group, *Homo sapiens*, meaning "wise man."

ANIMAL LIFE

Like plants, animals are made up of cells, usually many kinds of cells. Unlike plants, animals cannot make their own food. They have to eat plants or other animals for food. Also unlike plants, most animals are able to move around.

There are hundreds of thousands of different animal species. Some are tiny organisms smaller than specks of dust, but others are gigantic creatures, like elephants and whales. Elephants and whales—and humans—belong to the most advanced group of animals, the mammals. These animals give birth to live young, and the females feed their offspring with their milk.

Mammals and birds are warm-blooded. Their body temperature stays about the same in different surroundings. All the other animal groups, including fish, amphibians, and reptiles, are cold-blooded. Their body temperature changes with the temperature of their surroundings. All warm-blooded and some cold-blooded animals have bony backbones and are called vertebrates. Other types of animals in the animal kingdom do not have backbones and are called invertebrates.

HUMAN SUCCESS

Humans are not as big or as strong as many other animals, but they are the most intelligent. They have used their intelligence in many ways. By building shelters, they have been able to live nearly everywhere on Earth, from the scorching desert to the freezing Arctic. By inventing tools and building machines, they have been able to reshape their surroundings for their own survival.

Some people think that humans have become too successful. The world population is increasing rapidly. Humans are in danger of using up Earth's resources, such as fuels and minerals. They are also creating more and more pollution, which harms humans and other life-forms and damages Earth's atmosphere.

Earth is the only planet in the whole Universe where we know life exists. So humans have begun to look for ways to protect Earth and the unique life it contains.

Glossary

atmosphere: the layer of gases around Earth

aurora: colored lights that appear in the skies in far northern and southern parts of the world

axis: an imaginary line running through a planet from its north to its south pole

cell: the smallest unit of a living thing

climate: the yearly weather pattern of a region on Earth

continental drift: the gradual movement of Earth's land masses

crust: the hard outer layer of Earth

earthquake: shakings in underground rocks caused by movements in Earth's crust

erosion: the gradual wearing away of Earth's surface by the weather and other natural forces

evaporate: to change from liquid to vapor, or gas

geology: the study of Earth; geologists are scientists who study Earth

gravity: the attraction, or pull, that every heavenly body has on things on or near it

igneous rock: rock formed when magma cools

kingdom: a major grouping of living things, such as the plant kingdom and the animal kingdom

magma: molten, or liquid, rock

mantle: the layer of rock underneath Earth's crust

metamorphic rock: new rock formed when existing rock is altered by heat and pressure

meteorology: the study of the weather

minerals: solid substances in Earth that make up rocks

orbit: the path in space of one heavenly body around another

photosynthesis: the process by which plants make their food

planet: a large heavenly body that orbits the Sun

plate: one of the slabs of hard rock that make up Earth's surface

species: a kind of living thing

terrestrial: like Earth

tides: the rise and fall in level of Earth's oceans, caused mainly by the gravity, or pull, of the Moon

volcano: a place where molten rock from underground forces its way to the surface

water cycle: the constant exchange of water between Earth's surface and atmosphere

water vapor: water in the form of a gas

weathering: the wearing away of the Earth's surface by the weather

Index

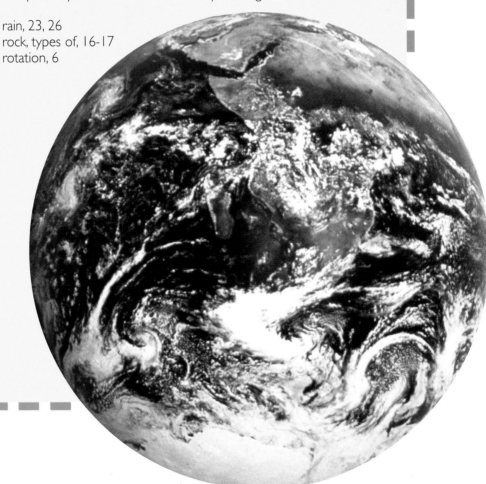